# D-DAY

*Operation Overlord: Cornwall & Preparation for the D-Day Landings*

– RODERICK DE NORMANN –

# TOR MARK

Published by Tor Mark Ltd,
United Downs Industrial Estate,
St Day, Redruth, Cornwall TR16 5HY

First published 2021, reprinted 2022

www.tormark.co.uk

ISBN 978 0 85025 454 9

Text: © Roderick De Normann, edited by Peter Blyth
Images: Cornish Studies Library, Critical Past: (www.criticalpast.com), Falmouth History Archive, via Royal Cornwall Polytechnic Society (RCPS), Ike Skelton Combined Arms Research Library, Tavistock Museum Archive, The Hyper Text Histories – HyperWar: (www.ibiblio.org/hyperwar), US Library of Congress - Prints and Photographs Online Catalog: (www.loc.gov/pictures), US National Archives & Records Administration – Archives Library Information Centre – Digital Photography Collections: (www.archives.gov/research/alic/reference/photography), US Naval History & Heritage Command (NHHC) - Photography: (www.history.navy.mil/our-collections/photography.html)

Printed and bound in the UK

## – A C K N O W L E D G E M E N T S –

Wartime history research in the United States is relatively easy. The vast majority of national files are both open to the public and free of charge. The latter is not so in the United Kingdom where exorbitant charges – especially for the use of photographs and film stills – means that only the wealthiest of authors and their publishers can afford to use them. So, it is to the United States that I say my first huge 'thank you'; the Library of Congress, the National Archives and Records Administration (NARA), the Naval History and Heritage Command (NHHC) and the US Navy 'Seabee' Museum. All have internet facilities that offer a huge array of photographs and documents, the majority of which are 'In the Public Domain' and are free to download.

In addition, the internet sensation at 'Fold3', part of Ancestry.com, is really quite outstanding. According to their own count, they have published some 519,491,559 records up to the time of writing.

In the same context, I must also thank Joe P. Harris of Absolutelyarchives, North Carolina, who trawled through endless NARA photographs on my behalf. In addition, I must also thank the staff at the Eisenhower Presidential Library who did their utmost to discover if General Eisenhower visited Cornwall prior to D-Day.

Back in Cornwall, I must thank the Falmouth History Archive – especially Peter Searle – who are part of the Royal Cornwall Polytechnic Society. At the Falmouth Maritime Museum, Captain (Retired) Hogg RN and Tony Pawlyn were both extremely helpful. Likewise, Kim Cooper and the staff at the Cornwall Studies Library, Redruth. The latter holds the Ellis Collection of wartime photographs, a real local archive treasure.

Finally, I must say thank you to Anna Corbett, my editor and mentor. After so long away from the writing and publishing world, her advice and guidance have been second-to-none.

**To one and all, many, many thanks.**

# – CONTENTS –

OMAHA BEACH, NORMANDY – *AT PRESENT*

*On the 5th June 1944, 38 Landing Ships (Tank) – or LSTs – departed from the Fal Estuary in South Cornwall. Others joined them from the Helford River, the port at Fowey and the River Tamar. Escorted by the Royal Navy and numerous American smaller craft, these LSTs were loaded with US soldiers of the 1st and 29th Infantry Divisions. Their destination was the landing beach in Normandy codenamed OMAHA.*

## - P R O L O G U E -

Following the attack on Pearl Harbour on the 7th December 1941, Britain declared war on Japan the following day, a few hours before the Americans themselves. Both were quickly followed by Canada and the Netherlands. Taken totally by surprise, Hitler issued an immediate order that the U-Boat fleet was to attack any US vessels they came across. This was three days before Germany and Italy officially declared war themselves on the United States. President Roosevelt of course, reciprocated.

American and British planning staffs began their work on Operations SLEDGEHAMMER and ROUNDUP in what Churchill reportedly described as '…marching ahead together in a noble brotherhood of arms…'. Meanwhile the Americans looked at the huge logistical problem of moving enough men and materiel into – or onto – the British Isles in an operation the Americans called BOLERO.

The American military logistics organisation that would oversee BOLERO was the Service of Supply (SOS), later renamed the Army Service Forces (ASF).

SOS-ETO (European Theatre of Operations), divided the UK into six Base Sections: Northern Ireland, Western (including Wales and Scotland), Eastern, Central around London, South Eastern and Southern. Southern Base Section (SBS) was to be where the bulk of US combat troops would be accommodated. SBS roughly stretched from Southampton, west to Land's End. SBS was itself divided into 13 districts, with Somerset, Devon and Cornwall making up the Western District, later renamed XIX District.

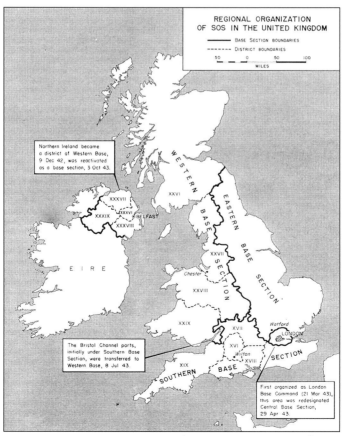

MAP – REGIONAL SOS COMMANDS (THE HYPER TEXT HISTORIES)

Each district within SBS was required to provide not only sufficient accommodation and storage space for the troops and their equipment once issued, but also sufficient space to store their heavier equipment.

Many of the existing British camps, barracks or garrisons within SBS were handed over to the Americans. Where military accommodation was not available, billeting was found in private homes. This was not difficult to find as the Americans paid just over $4.20 a day for the privilege, with many of those billeted able to supplement the meagre English rationing with excellent US Army supplies.

## {2} PLANNING AND PREPARATION FOR THE 'SECOND FRONT'

In 1942, Falmouth and Fowey were looked at in detail for receiving US Forces and their stores during BOLERO. Subsequently the UK Ministry of War Transport produced a report issued on the 25th July 1942. In Falmouth they had inspected the then King's, Empire and Queen's jetties alongside the road and rail facilities. Their conclusions were enlightening. The final report stated that:

*'In view of the present important use of the port and the limited rail facilities…Falmouth is not suitable…It might, however, be well regarded as a reserve port for use in an emergency when some temporary interference with ship repairs might have to be allowed.'*

For Fowey they looked at No.8 Jetty, then some 500ft long and purpose-built for the china-clay industry. It was, they noted, only able to accept cargo vessels drawing 25ft and who could discharge their own cargo. Rail facilities away from the harbour were good, but ran into a choke-point at Lostwithiel, as they did from Falmouth. Their conclusion was the same as that for Falmouth: of use but only in an emergency.

On the 7th October 1942, the same ROUND UP planning staff noted that in Falmouth and Fowey '…improvements to the facilities at these ports are well in hand…'. In the same report, the staff noted that there would be a requirement for 70 Landing Ship (Tank) (LST) and 150 for the smaller Landing Craft (Tank) (LCT) loading points or hard standings - 'hards'.

Initially it was British contractors who undertook the massive task of preparing the required facilities. With Falmouth and Fowey now being upgraded, locations for 'hards' were identified. These were primarily in Falmouth, along the River Fal, in the Helford River and on both banks of the River Tamar around Devonport and Plymouth. Today these are well known but back in 1942-1943 they were largely hewn out of new ground and their locations closely guarded. Each hard was given an identifying code. These - and their locations in Cornwall - were as follows:

| | | |
|---|---|---|
| PF-1 | Polgerran Wood, River Fal | 2 x LSTs |
| PF-2 | Turnaware Point, River Fal | 4 x LSTs |
| PF-3 | Harvey's Yard, Falmouth | 2 x LCTs |
| PF-4 | Taylor's Garage, Falmouth | 4 x LCTs |
| | | |
| PH | Polgwydden (Trebah), Helford River | 2 x LSTs |
| | | |
| PP-1 | Upper Barn Pool, Mt. Edgecombe | 4 x LSTs |
| PP-3 | Lower Barn Pool, Mt. Edgecombe | 4 x LCTs |
| PS | Jupiter Point, Devonport | 2 x LCTs |

Alongside all of the above, both the Prince of Wales Pier, Falmouth and Massack Point by St. Just-in-Roseland would also be used to embark troops onto Landing Ships Infantry (Large) (LSI(L))s.

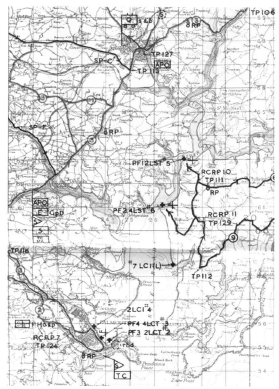

AN EXTRACT FROM THE OFFICIAL AMERICAN MAP OF THE FALMOUTH HARDS AND THE ROUTES INTO AND OUT OF THEM, PUBLISHED BY SOUTHERN BASE SECTION. (IKE SKELTON COMBINED ARMS RESEARCH LIBRARY)

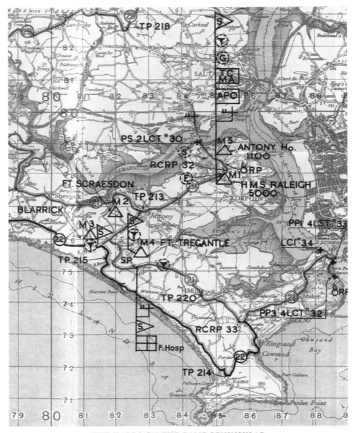

THE HARDS ON THE RAME PENINSULAR
(IKE SKELTON COMBINED ARMS RESEARCH LIBRARY)

The wartime biography of Bernard Breakell, a civilian Foreman of Works seconded to Falmouth by Plymouth Command, recalled that the building contract went to a London-based company 'Harbour and General Works Ltd'. They in-turn recruited a large force of over 100 workmen to prepare the sites and the 'hards'. These sloped gently into the water and covered the mean tide levels at both high and low water. LSTs and LCTs with their very shallow drafts were able to approach these points, lower their forward ramps and load or unload their cargoes.

The hards themselves were made up of flexible concrete matting resembling a chocolate bar, mass produced in moulds and usually in a configuration of 3 x 5 'pads'. Soon large dumps of this matting were to be seen at the designated points on the Fal. Jutting out from the hards were temporary jetties, known as 'dolphins'. These were little more than steel piles driven into the river bed with wooden gangways attached. Each 'dolphin' also had a water pipe – and in some cases a fuel pipe – incorporated for immediate replenishment. These piers would allow vessels to tie up alongside prior to loading or unloading.

The maritime operation to land the Allies on the beaches in northern France was 'Operation NEPTUNE'. All along the south coast, surveys had been completed and bases identified for future operations; in Cornwall the US Navy decided on Falmouth, St Mawes and Fowey. These were confirmed by the end of July 1943 and the agreements with the Royal Navy finalised. These would give the US Navy full freedom of action for command, organisation, training and support for their own forces. On the 28th July 1943 Admiral Stark, commanding NEPTUNE, informed the Navy Department in Washington that:

'...the British (are) to make available to us nearly all the housing, office and ship facilities that we need in Appledore, Falmouth, Fowey, Dartmouth, Salcombe, Teignmouth and Plymouth...the Royal Navy (will) supply...about 65% of naval stores, port machinery, boats, moorings etc, which we require. The requests on the United States for material (will be) kept to an absolute minimum'.

To ensure a suitable base and maintenance organisation, 'Landing Craft and Bases, Europe' or LANCRABEU, were established.

By the 1st June 1943, there were already 22,000 US Navy personnel stationed in the United Kingdom. The majority of these were based on Plymouth Command with 8,000 in Plymouth itself, 3,000 at Falmouth and 2,000 at Dartmouth. In addition, the US Navy built its primary naval ordnance depot at Exeter that needed 2,700 personnel to operate.

A US Naval Advanced Amphibious Base (USNAAB) was established at Falmouth, Cornwall. There were to be two sub-bases, one at St Mawes and another at Fowey. Prior to the main body of the base arriving from the US, an advance party under the command of Commander L.B. Ard from COMNAVEU had taken up residence in Falmouth and were overseeing the building of a camp on Beacon Hill, described by the Americans as '...part grazing land and [part] swampland...'.

COMMANDER JAMES E ARNOLD (USNR) AT HIS DESK IN THE HYDRO HOTEL, FALMOUTH (US NATIONAL ARCHIVES & RECORDS ADMINISTRATION)

US LANDING CRAFT VEHICLE (PERSONNEL) (LCV(P)) COME ASHORE AT SLAPTON SANDS. THESE VESSELS ARE LIKELY TO HAVE BEEN EITHER FROM ST MAWES OR FOWEY.
(US NAVY ARCHIVES VIA US NAVAL HISTORY & HERITAGE COMMAND)

Additionally, two USN Advanced Amphibious Training Sub-Bases (USNAATSB) were established at St. Mawes and Fowey, under base commanders Lieutenant Commanders Frank A. Varney and John P. Beale respectively. Their roles were to establish, train and then operate two landing craft flotillas, known as 'Standing Landing Craft Units' (SLCU) using the small Landing Craft, Vehicle (Personnel) (LCV(P)s and Landing Craft, Mechanised (LCM)s. These boats had a crew of four and were able to transport some 30 soldiers apiece, although the LCMs were also able to carry a medium tank. These craft were to be used in the final run-ups to the beaches in the initial waves of any landing. St. Mawes was to host SLCU-2 and Fowey SLCU-7.

LCVPS OF SLCU-2 IN ST MAWES HARBOUR AS PAINTED BY LIEUTENANT COMMANDER SHEPLER IN 1944.
(US NATIONAL ARCHIVES & RECORDS ADMINISTRATION – SHEPLER)

The initial US arrivals at all three bases went into the existing hotels and private houses. This was not as difficult as it first seemed due to the restrictions in the southern coastal belt. The Government banned indiscriminate travel in and out for some months either side of D-Day, freeing up the majority of the hotel rooms.

In Falmouth, the US Navy initially established its headquarters in the Greenbank Hotel, later moving it across the road to 4 Stratton Place. As personnel numbers increased, US officers remained billeted in the Greenbank Hotel, with the NCOs and Ratings using the King's Hotel, close to the Prince of Wales Pier. In addition, the Falmouth Hotel, Cliff Road and St. Michael's Hotel on Stracey Road were also requisitioned. The former was used to house senior US officers and the finance office. The latter was taken over as the US base hospital and dispensary. At the time, it was described as '…an up-to-date building with central heating, spacious grounds and excellent location'.

In St Mawes and Fowey, hotel accommodation and private houses were also used to begin with, although the official history of USNAATSB St Mawes revealed an odd twist to the tale. The Idle Rocks Hotel and the Ship & Castle Hotel were used for the enlisted men, while the officers were given the private houses Carricknath and Penmore. On arriving:

*'…all hands were immediately restricted to their quarters for a 48-hour period for the primary purpose of cleaning, fumigating and squaring-away [their] living quarters. The restriction made a remarkable impression on curious civilians, who were surprised to find that American sailors were not wholly undisciplined.'*

The offices for the Officer Commanding and his deputy were established in Carricknath, while the base was established at the then Bird's Boat Yard on the River Percuil.

LIEUTENANT COMMANDER DWIGHT SHEPLER, A US NAVY WAR ARTIST, SKETCHING, PROBABLY AT GROVE PLACE, FALMOUTH. SHEPLER WAS INITIALLY POSTED TO USNAAB FALMOUTH IN ORDER TO RECORD THE AMERICAN PRE-INVASION BUILD-UP TO D-DAY. ON THE 6TH OF JUNE, 1944 HE LANDED ON ONE OF THE OMAHA BEACHES. (US NAVAL HISTORY & HERITAGE COMMAND)

A LANDING CRAFT MECHANISED (LCM) EVACUATES LIGHTLY WOUNDED TROOPS FROM THE BEACHES IN NORMANDY, 6TH JUNE 1944. (US NAVY ARCHIVES VIA US NAVAL HISTORY & HERITAGE COMMAND)

NOTHING MUCH HAS CHANGED...FOWEY PLACE AND THE CHURCH OF ST FIMBARRUS ABOVE THE RIVER PACKED WITH US NAVY LANDING CRAFT AS PAINTED BY LIEUTENANT COMMANDER SHEPLER. (US NATIONAL ARCHIVES & RECORDS ADMINISTRATION – SHEPLER)

The harbours themselves also required considerable expansion. At Falmouth and Fowey, a large number of mooring lines needed to be provided for both large and small attack and landing craft alike. In Plymouth Command, the initial requirement was estimated to be 1,100 moorings and a similar number of berths both at anchor and alongside.

It was also anticipated that there would be a considerable requirement for both general and battle repair of vessels. The four Silley and Cox dry docks at Falmouth were ideal for major repairs and would be used extensively for the last two years of the war. For the smaller craft the US Navy took over Grove Place in Falmouth. Here they established a small maintenance base with a stores complex. In St. Mawes, Bird's Yard was taken over and at Fowey a new complex was built from scratch on the beach below Mixtow House. Alongside some of these smaller bases – at Falmouth, Mylor and Fowey – a series of simple low concrete piers evenly spaced 12 feet apart were constructed, the first two locations by E. Thomas and Son. Known as 'grids', these piers were set into the beach midway between high and low water. They worked by floating the flat-bottomed landing craft – anything from the smaller LCV(P)s to the larger LCTs - over the piers and securing them there until left high and dry by the receding tide.

A LARGE QUONSET HUT USED FOR REPAIRING BOTH US AND UK LCMS AND LCVPS AT GROVE PLACE, FALMOUTH. (ROYAL CORNWALL POLYTECHNIC SOCIETY, FALMOUTH HISTORY ARCHIVE)

FOLLOWING ON FROM OPERATION TORCH LST-325 ENTERS DRY DOCK AT FALMOUTH IN DECEMBER 1943 FOLLOWING HER SERVICE IN NORTH AFRICA AND SICILY. AFTER D-DAY, FALMOUTH DOCKS WERE ALMOST EXCLUSIVELY TURNED OVER TO SHIP REPAIR. (US NAVAL HISTORY & HERITAGE COMMAND)

'...AND THEY ENTERED TWO BY TWO...' – THE SHEER SIZE OF THE DRY DOCKS AT FALMOUTH MADE THEM IDEAL FOR FAST SHIP REPAIR. HERE LSTS–325 AND 356 IN DRY DOCK AT FALMOUTH DURING DECEMBER 1943 FOLLOWING THEIR ARRIVAL FROM THE MEDITERRANEAN.

Within the somewhat ad hoc US system, SLCU-2 was the first US Navy NEPTUNE unit to arrive in Cornwall, establishing itself in St Mawes on the 17th August 1943. Under the command of Lieutenant (jg) Paul J. Raab, the flotilla was formerly commissioned into service on the 7th September. The unit itself consisted of 20 officers and 60 four-man boat crews, a total of 240 NCOs and ratings. Alongside the SLCU, there were an additional 67 administrative and 'commissionary' (NAAFI) staff. This included a Red Cross shop that occupied the upper floors of the waterfront garage, today the St Mawes Gig Club and Village History Society. Initially the base only manned 18 LVC(P)s and six LCMs but almost immediately these were operating in ship to shore training onto Pendower Beach in Gerrans Bay.

For SLCU-7 in Fowey things were more complicated in that there was no accommodation ready for them. After an initial review by Lieutenant (jg) Heminway Merriman on behalf of COMNAVEU on the 24th August 1943, a detachment of the US Navy's 29th Construction Battalion arrived on the 16th September to start converting the hotels and houses to the improved standards required by the Americans. Soon after, and prior to SLCU-7, a naval maintenance and repair unit (known as an 'E-10' team) occupied Mixtow House. USNAATSB Fowey went on to be commissioned on the 25th October and it was only then that SLCU-7, codenamed 'AJEP-29', arrived in Fowey on the 3rd November 1943. The flotilla consisted of some 21 Officers and 225 NCOs and ratings under the command of Lieutenant Wilton Wenker. Initially only six landing craft were provided and these were sailed in from Plymouth. Akin to SLCU-2, training started almost immediately, using Crinnis and Pentuan beaches for small-boat training. Their first exercise – 'Operation No.1' – was held on the 7th November 1943, only four days after the flotilla's arrival at its new base.

Although detachments of the 29th CB had been upgrading requisitioned civilian buildings since mid-September, it would be the 81st CB that would make itself at home in all three Cornish bases. The battalion arrived in the UK in two tranches, being complete by the 5th October 1943, when it sent detachments down to Cornwall to relieve the 29th CB. In Cornwall the work undertaken was impressive and is best summed up thus:

| | |
|---|---|
| Falmouth | Built two 750-man hutted camps |
| | Erected one 1,000-man tented camp |
| | Converted St. Michael's Hotel into a hospital |
| St Mawes | Built one 264-man hutted camp for USN Ratings |
| | Upgraded twelve civilian buildings, including two hotels |
| Fowey | Built a 1,000-man hutted camp |
| | Built a separate 500-man hutted camp |
| | Built a 150-bed hospital |

The detachments of the 81st CB would remain in the Falmouth area until D-Day as they were re-rolled prior to the invasion. That said, while the US Navy trained, the CBs continued to work on the camps. In the end, they would spend four months working in Fowey and five months in both Falmouth and St Mawes.

With their camps being built around them, the US Navy got down to the task in hand. On the 13th October 1943 USNAAB Falmouth was officially commissioned and given the specific task of ensuring that the navy afloat was totally cared for. The men and their craft whose role was to transport the landing forces across to northern France were to want for nothing. Training programmes were organised, catering for all – from individual ratings all the way up to complete flotillas of LSTs or LCTs. Alongside all of this, Falmouth was also a major way point for vessels making their way to other south coast ports, be they from the US, the Mediterranean or just down from the bases in Londonderry or Rosneath. For the Americans, all of this had to be achieved in a very short time, from scratch and with the complete agreement of the Royal Navy's Plymouth Command. Contemporary US reports and accounts openly admit this was not necessarily so easy.

The Falmouth base history written in October 1944 noted two other problems. First, was the '...*impractical landscape of the average English town...there was very little centralization...*'. The report went on to note that it was two miles from the naval camp at Beacon Hill down to the main maintenance base at Grove Place or the Headquarters in the Hydro Hotel. Second, the USNAAB command had also to act as a reception base. This was, in due course, to become very difficult barely three months before the invasion.

As with Falmouth, the US training sub-bases at St Mawes and Fowey expanded rapidly. St Mawes was overcrowded almost immediately the Americans arrived there, with 70 officers and 596 NCOs and ratings 'on board' and by the end of January 1944, they were manning some 41 LCV(P)s and 38 LCMs. Such a large fleet necessitated that Bird's Yard had to be extended into a sizeable boat maintenance and repair facility. Initially a local contractor had built a steel refuelling and mooring pier but then a detachment of the 81st CB was ordered to sizeably extend the yard. Their efforts are still visible today; large concrete sea walls were built on the shingle beach and back-filling produced a sizeable hard-standing. Etched into the top of one of the concrete walls by one of the CBs are the words '81st "Seabees" Construction Battalion', proud testament to those hectic days.

CB 'FORMAL GRAFITTI' 74 YEARS ON. A NEATLY INSCRIBED REMINDER THAT THE 81ST 'SEABEES' WERE IN ST MAWES. (RODERICK DE NORMANN)

In addition to all the requisitioned hotels and houses, the 'Seabees' were detailed off in St Mawes to build a 200-bed hutted camp. The Americans chose a vacant field in front of a house called 'Varth' high-up on the point across today's Freshwater Lane. This in itself was not without problems as the unit war diary recounts:

*'The owner, a local lady, owned a sizable home and grounds across the road from the field. Her annoyance with the use of her land became one of the traditions of the base. Her objections were not so much to the despoiling of the land as to the fact that the structures interfered with her view of the Percuil River. So far as she was concerned her view was much more important than the progress of the war.'*

In Fowey, as with St Mawes, the US requirements also grew. Prior to the invasion, Fowey also became a naval training establishment. This came about after the first major exercise to test combined landing operations. SLCU-7 provided 24 LCV(P)s and 9 LCMs for Exercise DUCK I that landed on the live fire ranges at Slapton Sands further up the coast in Devon. This did not go well and it was decided that a serious amount of classroom instruction was required in all aspects of amphibious operations before further exercises were held. For the next few months, a vast array of both Army and Naval units went through the ad hoc schooling. Alongside this programme, additional instruction was given to both the landing craft flotilla and other small craft units in 'ship-to-shore' operations. This included instruction in handling palletised cargo and loose stores from LCTs and casualty evacuation. Additionally it was decided to establish a 'Hospital Corps Training School' on behalf of USNAAB Falmouth. Ultimately 150 officers and 2,850 hospital corpsmen would undertake the medical crash course and likely will have gone on to save many lives.

## {4} THE WESTERN TASK FORCE AND AMERICAN LANDING FORCES

The Allied plan for OVERLORD had a profound effect on Cornwall and its involvement with the future 'Second Front'. Up until the middle of 1943, the county had primarily been involved in supporting and training elements of the US Navy. Now there was an urgent need to base US soldiers into the county.

The Western Task Force – TF-122 – was the US naval force that would land the American 1st Army on the beaches in Normandy. The 1st Army was sub-divided by corps with V Corps assaulting Omaha and VII Corps landing on Utah. The former primarily consisted of the 1st, 2nd and 29th Infantry Divisions and the latter had the 4th, 9th, 79th and 90th Infantry Divisions. Alongside the assaulting infantry, a vast force of supporting arms, beach units and logistics were also going to land. Principal among these were the Engineer Special Brigade (ESB) groups. The 1st ESB was to land on Utah Beach and the 5th and 6th ESB to land on Omaha.

One of the first US divisions to arrive in the UK had been the 29th Infantry Division. The division was a National Guard unit and could trace its history back to the mid-eighteenth century. In the American Civil War, some of the original constituent units belonged to either Union or Confederate Forces. This is very much reflected in the divisional 'ying-yang' badge of dark blue and grey.

At that time, the 29th Infantry Division was composed of three infantry regiments, the 115th (1st Maryland), the 116th (The Stonewall Brigade) and the 175th (5th Maryland). In turn, each regiment was composed of three battalions, each composed of four rifle companies. In all, US regiments would number 3,118 men, with 871 in each of the battalions and 193 men in each of the companies. The divisional organisation also included artillery, engineer, ordnance and medical units. This was likewise reflected in both the regiments and the battalions where there were also detachments including administrative, medical and quartermaster personnel. In action, each regiment would form a combined arms Regimental Combat Team (RCT). For the 29th Division, these would be 115th, 116th and 175th RCTs. By June 1944 the Division had spent so much time in the UK that they were nicknamed 'England's Own'.

In moving down to the South West at the beginning of June 1943, the majority of the 29th Division were stationed in Cornwall. The locations for the larger units in October 1943 were noted as follows, less 116th RCT that was under command the 1st Infantry Division in Devon:

| | |
|---|---|
| Headquarters, 115th Regiment | Bodmin |
| 1st Battalion, 115th Regiment | St. Austell |
| 2nd Battalion, 115th Regiment | Scorne Cross, Launceston |
| 3rd Battalion, 115th Regiment | Bodmin |
| | |
| Headquarters 175th Regiment | Pendarves Estate, Camborne |
| 1st Battalion, 175th Regiment | St. Ives |
| 2nd Battalion, 175th Regiment | Helston |
| 3rd Battalion, 175th Regiment | Penzance |
| | |
| 29th Reconnaissance Troop | Fort Scraesdon |
| A Company, 104th Medical Battalion | Bodmin |
| C Company, 104th Medical Battalion | Clowence Estate, Camborne |
| 110th Field Artillery Battalion | Bodmin |

In July 1943, the division received a new commander, Major General Charles Hunter Gerhardt. Prior to his arrival in the West Country, a senior staff officer is claimed to have offered Gerhardt three pointers prior to his first senior command outside of America. He was advised that first, the 29th was likely to require serious amphibious training as it was undoubtedly to become involved in any future landings in Northern France. Second, the General was advised that he must be aware of Viscountess Astor living in Plymouth, a notable Virginian lady, she had married into the British aristocracy on her second marriage and had also become a British Member of Parliament for the seat of Plymouth Sutton. Thirdly, that the 29th were a National Guard division and that their discipline would unlikely be up to the standard of regular troops. This latter point must have wrankled with Gerhardt '...a West Pointer, an old cavalryman and avid polo-player...a disciplinarian of the old school...'. Although General Gerhardt did not disappoint, his first order to his new division was to give them three days holiday.

MAJOR GENERAL CHARLES H GERHARDT TOOK COMMAND OF THE 29TH INFANTRY DIVISION IN JULY 1943, LEADING THEM ALL THE WAY TO GERMANY. (TAVISTOCK MUSEUM ARCHIVE)

In Cornwall it was found that Bodmin Moor was ideal for training. There was plenty of freedom for soldiers to dig, vehicles to be driven and guns to be fired. At Berry Down, close to St. Neot, artillery positions were established in order to fire onto the crags at Brown Willy, some seven miles away. In other areas, the remains of engine houses and their chimneys made excellent targets or, as with the Black Dog Shaft at Wheal Busy, Chacewater, an area for explosives demolition training.

As for Lady Astor, Gerhardt was charming and would always have the upper hand as he had access to fresh meat and vegetables. She would regale him and his senior officers with stories from her youth in Virginia or with local jokes. After Lady Astor took part in a divisional talent show, Gerhardt presented her with a pig painted head to toe in blue and grey, pertaining to one of her jokes. Besides the pig, Lady Astor was made an honorary private in the Division, rising to sergeant and ultimately becoming a second lieutenant by the end of the war.

VICOUNT AND VICOUNTESS ASTOR PRIOR TO WORLD WAR 2. NANCY ASTOR STOOD FOR THE SEAT OF PLYMOUTH SUTTON AND WON, ENTERING PARLIAMENT IN 1919, THE FIRST WOMAN TO DO SO. SHE RELINQUISHED HER SEAT IN 1945. (US LIBRARY OF CONGRESS)

While the vast majority of Americans were polite, humble and more than appreciative of their time in the UK, there were occasions that exposed a number of problems. Primary amongst these was the inherent racist attitudes of particularly the southern born white troops against any black SOS units. Segregation was the order of the day with approximately 85% of white troops supporting it alongside only 48% of black troops. Unfortunately, the latter tended to be only allowed to have access to the more inferior facilities. An added problem was the attitude of the locals around the bases. They saw no problems in seeing either black or white troops in their pubs, clubs and dances, infuriating a minority of the white Americans.

SOS TROOPS WERE OFTEN AFRICAN-AMERICANS; FULLY ACCEPTED BY THE BRITISH BUT REJECTED BY A A MINORITY OF US TROOPS. WITHOUT THEM, HOWEVER, SOS AND ITS OPERATION NEPTUNE LOGISTICS PLAN WOULD NOT HAVE GONE AS SMOOTHLY AS IT DID. (CRITICAL PAST)

This discomfiture went right to the top, through General Eisenhower to President Roosevelt. Many orders were issued to try and quell the problems but they kept bubbling to the surface, on occasion leading to open street battles. In Launceston on the night of the 26th September 1943, a new SOS unit that included a large number of African-American troops were incensed when they were not allowed to drink in the same pubs as white troops. Later that evening, a group of the former returned armed with an array of weaponry, including rifles and Tommy Guns. A struggle ensured and two Military Policemen were wounded.

Any landing onto the beaches in Northern France would require serious cooperation of all the forces involved. Despite being fit and generally trained to use all their weapons and understand their tactics, the assault forces also needed to digest the complex coordination and sheer difficulties of landing on an open beach against a live enemy. New weapons and new tactics had to be devised, practised and then integrated into what would become the largest operation of its time.

In South Devon, the British Government requisitioned a long stretch of the coast between Strete and Torcross and all the farms inland up to a line between Blackawton and East Allington, in all some 30,000 acres. All residents and their livestock had six weeks to clear the area; 3,000 people and 180 farms. All village churches were carefully emptied of their artefacts, carvings and plate and their more precious architectural features protected under sandbags. The pubs, of course, were cleared of all their remaining stocks of beer and cider. As the locals moved out, the US Army moved in and established a live-fire range. The selected area needed to be so large, in order to cater for rounds that ricocheted or, as sometimes happened, fired at the wrong range or off the wrong sighting scale.

A FAMILY LEAVES ITS COTTAGE TO MAKE WAY FOR THE ALLIED AMPHIBIOUS LIVE-FIRE AREA BASED ON SLAPTON SANDS. (US NAVAL HISTORY & HERTIAGE COMMAND)

Slapton Sands had a number of useful similarities to what would likely be met on OMAHA Beach in Northern France. The general terrain was rugged and rose up to a bluff with many drainage lines onto the beach. In some areas there were cliffs and the beach mostly made up of shingle over sand. The tidal range was small, only 10-14ft, but enough to practise the US Navy in delivering troops by tides.

Before any exercise or operation there had to be some form of plan within which the assault troops could be marshalled into the correct order, for the correct ship and delivered at the correct time onto the correct beach.

This was to be the 'Mounting Plan' in support of Operation NEPTUNE. The British and the Americans agreed to three main points:

a. First, the initial assault waves onto the beaches must be as hard-hitting as possible. There would be no room for supporting troops and all such personnel would need to be stripped out and landed separately.

b. Second, the assaulting force needed to be composed of a varied number of experts in their specialist fields, not just 'bayonets'. Artillery observers, assault engineers, tanks and guns and the like would also need to be landed in well trained all-arms teams. They would need to be loaded onto the landing craft as they meant to get off.

c. Third, to achieve such aims, the assault force would require mustering and marshalling by boat load prior to moving to their embarkation hards for loading.

To ensure that such a plan worked, it was soon realised that the assault troops could not administer themselves. Prior to moving onto their landing craft and ships, they would have to be looked after within comfortable, sanitary conditions with more than adequate facilities within which they would be 'sealed' to ensure security. The next time they would disembark would be on the enemy coast. Such a plan necessitated one vital element - the date and time that the first waves would land. Everything else worked back from there.

The plan devised consisted of a number of phases through which the forces would flow. First was the home station phase, or the 'BOLERO installation' phase as the Americans initially called it. These were the barracks or camps that were home to the troops. It was here that the units would shake themselves out, the administrative personnel would be detached from the assault troops and the latter would digest their initial movement orders; vehicles were to be waterproofed and last minute logistical problems sorted out.

Second was the 'marshalling areas'. It was here that all the tactical and operational necessities would be catered for. It was also here that each individual soldier was to be briefed on the actual assault plan. Security was paramount so each and every marshalling area was 'sealed'; no one allowed out and no one allowed in. For the Americans, their own Military Police would cover the security within the marshalling area while the British police would cover the local civilian population. In all, the Americans would use 2,000 security personnel to patrol their camps.

Due to such tight security, every possible potential requirement that might be asked for was made available; food was plentiful, the beds comfortable, films and libraries laid-on. Last letters and wills were written with the US postal units handling some 10,500 sacks of mail out of the camps and 13,000 sacks in. This included the final issue of any personal requirements – anything from a new rifle to a new razor. Weapons and vehicles were given a last check that included a final drive through deep water filled pits in each area to check the waterproofing. It was also in these marshalling areas that each individual was issued with his lifebelt, personal rations, additional ammunition and three prophylactics. The majority of which ended up over personal watches, wallets and rifle muzzles. Each soldier was also issued 200 Francs in Allied 'invasion money, printed by the Allies to the everlasting fury of General de Gaulle. The US exchange rate was 2 US cents to the franc!

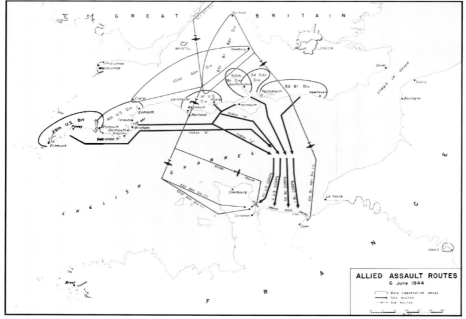

OPERATION NEPTUNE MARSHALLING AREAS AND THEIR CONVOY ROUTES TO NORMANDY.
(THE HYPER TEXT HISTORIES)

A marshalling area included a number of troop holding camps and railheads for vehicles and stores. Each area had a designation letter, the British having Camps 'A', 'B' and part of 'C' while the Americans had the other part of 'C', 'D' and 'K' to 'O'. In Cornwall, the US troops were marshalled in the majority part of 'M', located on the Cornish side of the Tamar opposite Plymouth and in areas 'N' and 'O'. These latter two areas were based on the embarkation hards around Falmouth and Helford.

THE INTERIOR OF PROBABLY ONE OF THE CAMPS WITHIN SAUSAGE O–D, RUNNING NORTH–EAST OUT OF HELSTON. (CRITICAL PAST)

These marshalling areas were administered by districts within the SBS, in particular Districts XVIII and XIX. The commandant of the latter was Colonel Theodor Wyman Jr, a regular army engineer. He was tasked with providing suitable marshalling camps for the 29th Infantry Division and the assorted attached 1st Army assault troops. His plan was very simple – to take over many of the back roads and build the camps alongside these. The roads would provide the vehicle hard standings while in the adjacent fields temporary tented camps were erected.

On a map, these long ribbon camps appeared as 'sausages' and hence they were all nicknamed 'sausage camps'. Some of these camps stretched a very long way, some over ten miles. Conversely, for 'M' Area, where many of the troops were based in large barracks with their embarkation points literally down the road, there was little need for 'sausage camps'.

A US JEEP FULLY LOADED AND WATERPROOFED FOR THE LANDINGS TRUNDLES PAST THE ENTRANCE TO A 'SAUSAGE CAMP'. THE BOARD IN THE BACKGROUND APPEARS TO READ 'D-7', SUGGESTING THIS IS ONE OF THE CAMPS OF 'O-D', LARGELY OCCUPIED BY ELEMENTS OF THE 175TH INFANTRY REGIMENT, 29TH INFANTRY DIVISION. (CRITICAL PAST)

A US 'SAUSAGE CAMP' IN CORNWALL. THE LENGTH OF THE FILM SEQUENCE SUGGESTS IT MIGHT BE CAMP F OF MARSHALLING AREA O BASED IN CHACEWATER, CORNWALL. (CRITICAL PAST )

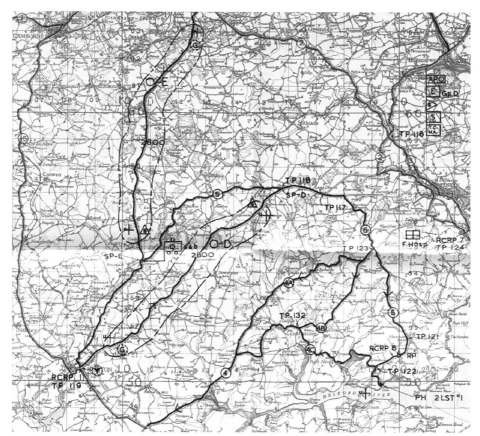

MARSHALLING CAMPS O-D AND O-E WERE BOTH LINKED TO THE EMBARKATION HARDS AT POLGWYDDEN (TREBAH) ON THE HELFORD RIVER. (IKE SKELTON COMBINED ARMS RESEARCH LIBRARY)

The final phase was embarkation. This was to begin on 'Load (L)-Day' and would be in direct relation to 'D-Day'. With everything and everyone ready to go, unit convoys would move down to the embarkation points. Every soldier and vehicle had a place earmarked on each individual landing craft. All vehicles would be driven – backwards - onto either the LCTs or LSTs while the general infantry would be shipped out to their LCI(L)s off-shore.

Just as there was a detailed and intricate plan for the ground assault troops, there was a similar plan for the naval units and vessels that were to carry them.

The plan devised outlined a number of phases for each landing craft. These worked on the premise that each vessel would move from its home port to its designated loading hard, load, move to its convoy forming-up point and finally, sail for Normandy.

TROOPS EMBARKING ONTO LSI(L)S AT THE PRINCE OF WALES PIER, FALMOUTH. THIS IS LIKELY TO BE FOR EXERCISE DUCK I ON THE 30TH DECEMBER 1943. THE MAJORITY WEAR THEIR OVERCOATS AND CARRY THEIR BEDDING ROLES, ITEMS NOT CONDUCIVE TO STORMING A BEACH. (CRITICAL PAST)

A plan such as this covered many square miles and relied on the ability for the troops and their vehicles to move at the right time to the right point. As a result, the Americans established two huge road networks, one 16ft wide, the other 22ft wide; these roads were subsequently closed to all civilian traffic. Should any stretch of road not be of sufficient width, US engineers moved in and widened it. This was usually achieved by scraping back the verges and placing a layer of concrete over the top. Many of these patches are still visible today.

Traffic was regulated and all one-way along particular routes. Virtually every cross-road or major turn had a traffic post and, in order to avoid any blockage, a large number of vehicle recovery and repair units were established throughout the network. Any vehicle that did breakdown was removed from the road and a replacement whistled-up if it could not be repaired quickly.

US CONVOY ON A WIDENED CORNISH ROAD, LINED WITH AMMUNITION STORAGE BUNKERS JUST PRIOR TO D–DAY 1944. (CRITICAL PAST)

TRUCKS MOVE THROUGH MAWNAN SMITH UNHINDERED. 'TP 121' STANDS FOR 'TRAFFIC POINT 121' AND WOULD HAVE BEEN MANNED BY THE AMERICAN FIELD SERVICE (AFS) STANDING IN THE ROAD. NOTE THE RED LION PUB AT THE TOP OF THE ROAD. (CRITICAL PAST)

There are three basic tenets for military operations at all levels. The first states that any exercise or rehearsal for battle should be more gruelling, more difficult and perhaps more dangerous, than the future action itself. The second states that any military plan will disintegrate on first contact with the enemy. The third that time spent in reconnaissance is seldom wasted. Running into a series of large-scale exercises, the Americans ran afoul of these at some time or other, sometimes all three at once.

With the 'Mounting Plan' in place all the planners were very keen to test it and iron out any problems. Although many of the troops were highly trained, large elements of the ultimate plan had yet to be tested. All of these would lead onto two major D-Day rehearsals, exercises FABIUS for the OMAHA landings and TIGER for those onto UTAH. This was particularly so with regards to the naval forces embarking troops and landing them, linking in the SLCUs at St. Mawes and Fowey with the troop-carrying convoys and coordinating both the air and sea bombardments to cover the landings. With the establishment of an Assault Training Centre at Woollacombe and the live-fire exercise and ranges at Slapton Sands, the time was now ready to see what worked and what did not.

The first major exercise was written and planned in late 1943 to be undertaken in early January 1944: 'Exercise DUCK I'. Due to the firing of live ammunition and the security implications, the Americans deemed such exercises as 'operations'.

The aim of this first foray was to practise the mounting of a landing, from concentration area to embarkation. Exercise control was with Headquarters XIX District and was broken down into two phases – the mounting and the landing. Royal Navy elements would provide real-time protection from both submarine and E-Boat attack and the IX US Air Force would provide protection in the air.

The first troops exercised in DUCK I were from the 175th Infantry Regiment and the 1st Engineer Special Brigade. With them went a number of headquarter teams including one from the IX US Air Force and another from V Corps, both supported by the 56th Signal Battalion. The exercising troops were spread far and wide, from Helston to Taunton and embarkation was to take place in both Falmouth and Dartmouth. During the beach landing, some 10,242 men would be exercised and 1,096 vehicles of all types landed, with another 10,156 men from SBS units employed to actually run the exercise.

As the troops left their concentration areas they moved into temporary camps established in the Helston, Falmouth, Redruth, Truro and St. Austell areas with another way to the east, at Lupton House near Dartmouth. These camps preceded the future marshalling areas that came later. Each area had 14 tented camps and parking for 1,000 vehicles. The initial landing was planned for the 3rd of January, 1944 but was delayed until the following day, the 4th.

US CONVOY CONTROL JEEP OF THE 29TH INFANTRY DIVISION PATIENTLY WAITS TO BE CALLED FORWARD TO EMBARK PRIOR TO D–DAY, C.DECEMBER 1943 DURING EXERCISE DUCK 1. (CRITICAL PAST)

ORDERS WERE ISSUED THAT ALL VEHICLES WERE TO BE FULLY FUELLED AT ALL TIMES. (CRITICAL PAST)

Incorporated into DUCK I were a number of logistic tasks to be considered and tested. To move the considerable quantities of stores that would be required to support the troops, four British coasters were pre-loaded in Bristol on the 24th December with ammunition, fuel and rations. These were 'skid-loaded' – palletised in today's parlance – for the first time.

The troops landed on the dot at 10.00am on the 4th January, but almost immediately things went awry. Some naval craft came ashore in the wrong waves and the inshore ley caused problems for the troops moving inland as bridging failed to arrive on the beach on time. The Special Engineers landed 25 minutes after the assault troops and immediately began to clear the beach of mines as per their orders but while other troops were landing. In the afternoon, the four British coasters arrived and their cargoes offloaded into either one of the LCMs or into a DUKW, an amphibious truck. Throughout the time on the beach, the Americans tested any number of ideas for waterproofing supplies. Such tactics included the skid-loads, track-laying and large tannoys with which to relay commands across the beach or out to sea. The exercise lasted two days before all troops packed up and returned to barracks by XIX District.

LST-325 LANDED AND OFFLOADED ELEMENTS OF THE 29TH INFANTRY ONTO SLAPTON SANDS, DEVON DURING EXERCISE DUCK I HELD IN EARLY JANUARY 1944. (US NATIONAL ARCHIVES & RECORDS ADMINISTRATION)

During the whole affair, there were any number of observers taking notes and seeing what was or was not working. The first exercise critique was held at V Corps Headquarters on the 12th January and at XIX Headquarters on the 20th and 26th. All agreed that DUCK I was a credible success as a first attempt. All agreed that the initial marshalling was excellent but there was a number of problems noted. One of the more worrisome threads running through the whole exercise was the obvious lack of tactical training displayed by the supporting troops landing behind the assault. This was especially so with the Special Engineers many of whom had actually participated in landings in Sicily and Italy during 1943. The average unloading time for the LSTs was ten hours, not the five required. Many also had incomplete manifests so that the beach masters had little idea of who or what was in each ship.

DUCK I was quickly followed by DUCKs II and III, importantly, establishing a centralised planning staff.

Exercise TIGER was the UTAH Beach equivalent of FOX, a rehearsal of a rehearsal. What made TIGER different from FOX was that a large number of very senior visitors had planned to observe the exercise. These included Generals Eisenhower, Montgomery and Bradley, the overall naval commander Admiral Ramsey and the Air Force Commander, Air Marshal Tedder. With them were a large number of others from General Eisenhower's headquarters. All were keen to see the initial exercise serials, the RAF Typhoon fighter-bombers strafing and using their 60lb rockets as well as the initial run in to the beach by the amphibious DD Sherman tanks.

Unfortunately all was not well. LCTs of the US Navy fell behind time and the opening sequences were delayed by an hour. This was not relayed to all the assault forces and the second wave landed on time, before the first wave. With troops on the beaches, the planned bombardments had to be cancelled but here reality becomes conjecture. There are a number of eye witness accounts that quite clearly recall navy shells landing on the beach while it was still occupied by troops. Rumours at the time say upwards of 450 soldiers were killed but this is doubtful. If rounds did land on the occupied beach, the firing would have been stopped almost immediately.

All day things went wrong, were delayed or simply did not happen. Many of the senior observers were far from impressed when three LCTs, equipped with over 1,000 rockets each, came in and fired inland at a series of barbed wire and pill box targets. Once the smoke cleared it was obvious that many had fallen short, with the smoke and dust blowing out to sea in the off-shore wind, totally obscuring the vision of the launching DD tanks. Problems continued and in full view of the senior officers, one of the DD tanks promptly sank.

If the day was going badly, the night turned decidedly nasty. German S-Boats armed with torpedoes, cannon and machine-guns caught a convoy sailing along the coast at night. Two LSTs were sunk and another very badly damaged. In 1946, the official casualty figures were given as 749 killed and 300 wounded, with many of the latter suffering exposure from having been in the sea for a considerable time before rescue.

Many of those who died served within 1st ESB. This brigade had been swapped with the 6th ESB. Of their sub-units, the 3206th Quartermaster Service Company was virtually wiped out, with the official report claiming 201 killed from a full complement of 250 officers and men. Another badly hit unit was the 557th Quartermaster Railhead Company who reportedly suffered 69 casualties in total. Unfortunately, some of the casualties were due to Americans firing at Americans. LST-511 was badly hit by 20mm fire from LST-496 that had steamed off to a flank. The majority of the wounded suffered badly having been hit by these large-calibre rounds.

The final rehearsals for the landings was a series of six planned exercises called FABIUS I to FABIUS VI. These were to cover four of the five assaults and the two follow-up forces, although the UTAH Beach landing was not exercised due to TIGER. Exercises FABIUS I to IV were held simultaneously between the 23rd April and the 7th May under command of Headquarters, 21st Army Group. FABIUS V and VI were held between the 4th and 6th May, coinciding with the landings of the previous four. FABIUS I involved the US 1st and 29th Infantry Division elements that were to land on OMAHA Beach. The landings again took place on Slapton Sands.

What set FABIUS aside from all the other exercises was that it was designed to test the complete invasion infrastructure not the assault forces. The exercises were to resemble Operation NEPTUNE as closely as possible in order to ensure that the higher echelons were tested. The biggest difference from what went before was that the assault troops did not return to their old barracks or concentration areas, instead returning to the marshalling camps. Lessons were learnt but time was running out.

On the 8th May 1944, the Supreme Allied Commander Europe (SACEUR), General Eisenhower, set D-Day for the 5th June.

Between March and June 1944, the West Country quite literally filled up with US troops. Cornwall bore the brunt. Tented camp after tented camp sprang up around Truro and yet more houses and their grounds were requisitioned as continuous streams of men and supplies were squeezed into the county.

Alongside the large exercises FOX, TIGER and FABIUS, other smaller exercises were also ordered on more local beaches. This was particularly important for the US Naval Combat Demolition Units (NCDU) based first in Falmouth and then Fowey.

In February 1944 USN beach intelligence reported, for the first time, obstacles being constructed on the landing beaches in Normandy. These were being built at the mid-point between the spring and neap tide lines and were obviously designed to counter landing craft. Some of these were very basic, merely pit props with an anti-tank mine or artillery shell attached to the end. Others were more devilish and designed to rip open the hulls of vessels below the waterline. Steel tetrahedrons – or 'hedgehogs' - and obstacles called 'Belgian Gates' were particularly worrisome and would require explosives through which to force gaps for the landing craft.

With the profusion of obstacles now appearing on the beaches – nicknamed 'Rommel's Asparagus' – additional teams were needed for their clearance. On the 30th April V Corps announced the formation of the counter obstacle group. This consisted of two Army engineer combat battalions, reinforced with Sherman tank bulldozers. These engineer battalions were split down into 21 Navy Combat Demolition Units (NCDU). Their task would be to clear all obstacles on the beaches within the defined lanes and below the high tide lines.

BELGIAN GATES, THE MOST SUBSTANTIAL OF ROMMEL'S BEACH DEFENCES, REQUIRED A TEAM OF FOUR TO DEAL WITH THEM. (CRITICAL PAST)

Between the 31st October 1943 and the 14th February 1944, ten of the new NCDU units arrived in the UK and were sent south to Falmouth. Here they were equally divided into Groups I, II and III and attached to the 7th, 6th and 2nd Beach Battalions, themselves attached to each assaulting Regimental Combat Team. Of these, Group III went to Fowey. Between late-February and mid-April, the Fowey NCDU teams were involved in considerable experimental work to clear the beach obstacles.

While at Fowey one of the NCDU commanders, Lt Hagensen, developed what became known as the 'Hagensen Pack Charge'. This was a 2lb block of the new C2 plastic explosive in a sown canvas bag with a basic lit fuse. These charges were designed for use against steel obstacles and were found to be very effective. Right up to the point where the NCDU teams went to their marshalling camps, sail-makers in Fowey were to be found hard at work sowing the bags for the explosives charges.

A US NAVAL COMBAT DEMOLITION TEAM TACKLES A 'HEDGEHOG' OBSTACLE – INK AND WASH DRAWING BY MITCHELL F. JAMIESON, 1944. THESE OBSTACLES COMPRISED OF THREE STEEL RAILS RIVETED IN THE MIDDLE WITH THE FEET SPLAYED TO PREVENT SINKING INTO THE SAND. (US NAVAL HISTORY & HERTIAGE COMMAND)

As the run-up to D Day fast approached, the south coast slowly braced itself. In Cornwall, the embarkation points were ready and the marshalling camps prepared. In Falmouth, St. Mawes, Fowey and Plymouth, the final US flotillas arrived from the Mediterranean and moored up.

In St. Mawes, SLCU-2 moved into their new hutted camp completed by the 81st Construction Battalion on the 25th April 1944. It was used on several Saturday nights for dances or ENSA and MSO musical shows. Towards the end of April, the base numbers began to decrease as sections were moved out to join the invasion fleet. This included 30 LCMs and crews that left for their assembly point at Southampton.

With everyone moving out, steps were taken to begin the decommissioning of the base; by the 28th July 1944 it was dismantled.

At Fowey in the run-up to D-Day, life was very busy. It had become an out-station of the US base at Plymouth. Not only did it support SLCU-7, it had become a major logistics hub and had been designated as a reception and initial rehabilitation centre for ship crews sunk at sea. Indeed, some of the first rescued crewmen were those rescued during Exercise TIGER. Its importance was emphasised by the visits from Admirals Stark, Kirk and Moon. All training had ceased and the vacated camps were turned over to these men. Given good and plentiful food, fresh milk and availability to varied recreational facilities, many began to quickly make the recovery to duty fitness. At the same time, the medical school at Fowey was also heavily involved in preparing for a major medical exercise, practising casualty treatment and evacuation from the beaches out to waiting ships. This was Exercise SPLINT and principally used the beach by Pentewan, in St Austell Bay.

EXERCISE SPLINT WAS DESIGNED TO TEST CASUALTY EVACUATION FROM A BEACH ONTO AN LST PRIOR TO EVACUATION. (US NATIONAL ARCHIVES & RECORDS ADMINISTRATION)

In Falmouth, greater and greater numbers of landing-craft of all types, big and small, moored up for their final preparations prior to embarkation. Falmouth, Helford, Fowey and Plymouth West were to load up Task Force 126 or 'Follow-on Force B', destined to land additional troops onto both the beaches at OMAHA and UTAH between the first and third tides. At the same time, many of the LSTs would be assigned to tow various elements of the proposed artificial breakwaters, causeways and the newly-designed Rhino Ferries and Tugs.

Each beach had two elements; the 'approach' and the 'beach' itself. The 'approach' constituted the part of the beach uncovered at 'low-water-springs' but covered at 'high-water-neaps' with the 'beach' being that which lies between 'high-water-springs' and 'high-water-neaps'. In order to land on the average beach, the standard LST was designed with a keel gradient of 1 in 50, 3 feet deep at the bow and 9 feet deep at the stern. Thus, on landing at a beach with a similar gradient, LSTs could off-load immediately. The selected Normandy beaches had an average 'approach' of nearly a quarter of a mile with a gradient of 1 in 300, with the 'beach' having a gradient of 1 in 40. As such, assault landings could only really be undertaken during the high-water of Spring tides. Any other tides would mean that LSTs would run their sterns aground with eight feet of water at the bow. Consequently, some form of floating platform was required to cover the last 300 yards or so, referred to as the 'watergap'.

The concept behind the Rhino Ferry (RHF) was a 'pontoon', a water-tight floating steel box measuring 7ft x 5ft x 5ft and called a T6 Naval Lighterage (NL) unit. The first shipment of pontoons arrived in the country on the 15th November and a detachment of the 81st CB in Falmouth was set to work to build the first ferry, a Rhino Tug, later numbered 'RHT-1'. This was finished just after the 1st December whereupon production of the first Rhino Ferry immediately started. The Falmouth construction yard was alongside the 'hards' at Harvey's Timber Yard.

A RHINO TUG (RHT) UNDER CONSTRUCTION IN FALMOUTH. THESE TUGS USED SPECIALLY DESIGNED ENGINE UNITS WHILE THEIR LARGER COUSINS, THE RHINO FERRIES, USED MORE SUBSTANTIAL OUTBOARD ENGINES. (US NATIONAL ARCHIVES & RECORDS ADMINISTRATION)

For D-Day, 27 tugs and ferries were completed by the 25th April. At the same time, the Americans began an experimental programme looking at floating causeways, starting at the beginning of February 1944. This was undertaken in Par Harbour with the causeways designed to allow shallow-draft vessels to unload dry-shod.

In the middle of May 1944, the 29th Infantry Division, its attached support units and the accompanying Engineer Special Brigade Group units moved into their Marshalling Areas. Many believed this was yet another exercise but others noted the tighter security and sheer weight of troops and equipment in evidence. The units within their camps were split up into their boatloads. With this came the detailed briefings although, in most cases, the real names of towns along with their grid references were not given with final orders only opened onboard the landing craft.

One major problem solved at the last moment was the lack of personnel to service the assaulting troops in the 'sausage camps', particularly cooks and logistics staff. After much strife, it was decided to order the 5th US Armoured Division into Cornwall from Wiltshire to assist in running the camps. After arriving in the UK during February 1944, the 5th Armoured moved into the camps around Truro, Plymouth and Torquay in early April 1944.

When not looking after those in the camps as they moved onto the embarkation hards, the 5th Armoured Division personnel were allowed local leave into towns such as Redruth, Truro and Chacewater with the local population opening up their evening clubrooms for those off-duty soldiers.

THE BOSCOWEN (L) AND PENTARGON (R) HOTELS, FALMOUTH, BOMBED IN THE EARLY HOURS OF THE 30TH MAY 1944, KILLING FIVE AND WOUNDING 15. (CORNISH STUDIES LIBRARY)

On the night of the 29th and 30th May, 30 German bombers attacked Falmouth in what was to be the last raid of the war in the county. In all, some 30 metric tons of bombs were dropped.

Several bombs hit important targets. The Pentargon and Boscowen Hotels received direct hits, killing five and wounding 18. Ironically the Headquarters of the RAF's 959 Barrage Balloon Squadron in Falmouth was badly damaged next door. Outside of the town, the Swanpool oil and fuel installation was also hit. One of the fuel tanks ruptured and immediately caught fire, spilling burning oil into a local stream close to a row of houses. The fire burned for 22 hours, despite all the efforts by both the Falmouth Fire Brigade and US naval volunteers, some of whom were from the USNAAB Fire Fighting Team. Two US bulldozers were brought in to dam-up the stream for which the two US operators were awarded the British Empire Medal. One of the recipients, Bosun's Mate Philip Bishop, went on to marry a local Cornish lady.

THE SWANPOOL OIL AND FUEL INSTALLATION BURNING AFTER THE GERMAN RAID IN THE EARLY HOURS OF 30TH MAY 1944. IT TOOK MANY MEN AND MANY HOURS TO BRING UNDER CONTROL (US NATIONAL ARCHIVES & RECORDS ADMINISTRATION)

In the surrounding countryside, now packed with marshalled troops waiting to board their landing craft from their 'sausage camps', a large bomb hit the temporary garage of the 3516th Ordnance Medium Automobile Maintenance Company, that had been undertaking immediate vehicle repairs for those troops waiting to load. The single bomb killed five and wounded another three while they slept.

BOSUN'S MATE PHILLIP BISHOP PHOTOGRAPHED AS HE DAMS THE RUNNING RIVULETS OF BURNING FUEL–OIL POURING FROM A RUPTURED TANK AT SWANPOOL (US NATIONAL ARCHIVES & RECORDS ADMINISTRATION)

Despite the worsening weather, L-Day for embarkation remained the 31st May 1944. Follow-on Force B, known as Task Force 126 (TF-126), was made up of troops due to land on both OMAHA and UTAH immediately behind the assault force. Commanded by Commodore C.D. Edgar and based out of Plymouth, TF-126 consisted of four convoys; three 'slow' travelling at five knots and one fast, travelling at 12 knots. Convoys B-1 out of Plymouth and Fowey, B-3 from Falmouth and Helford and U-4 from Salcombe in Devon were 'slow'. This was due to having to tow Rhino Ferries or Tugs, Causeway sections and Gooseberry or Mulberry Harbour elements across the Channel. Convoy B-2 was a fast convoy, leaving from Plymouth on D-day itself. All four convoys were due to sortie-out at D minus 1 (D-1) with B-1 heading for Utah and B-2 for Omaha.

Both were due to be off-shore by the 2nd tide on D-Day. B-3 and U-4 were to merge off Salcombe and became Convoy ECL-1. Although each individual vessel within the convoy had a designated beach which to approach, this was to be confirmed at the time.

Loading Force B was a complicated business due to the number of harbours being used. LST loading was split into four Loading Groups, from A to D. Each ship was ordered to sail to a holding harbour prior to being called forward to its hard. Once loaded, the vessel was directed to a mooring position in the harbour from which it would sail. At each hard LST loading was further broken down in to groups, with each vessel given only six hours to embark its assigned loads. Each Cornish 'hard' loaded the following LSTs:

Polgerran Wood, River Fal (PF-1):
- Group A - LSTs 54, 212, 497, 5 and 386.
- Group B - LSTs 61, 307, 292, 393 and 306.

Turnaware Point, River Fal (PF-2):
- Group A – LSTs 331*, 392, 355, 7 and 356.
- Group B – LST 389.
- Group C – LSTs 391 and 53.
- Group D – LSTs 523, 59, 338, 325 and 336.

Helford River, Falmouth (PH):
- Group A – LSTs 532, 27*, 266, 369, 335 and 516.
- Group B – LSTs 28, 533, 262*, 538, 16* and 337.

Upper Barnpool, Plymouth (PP-1):
- Group A – LSTs 495, 494, 55, 498, 291, 496 and 512.
- Group B – LSTs 288, 504, 56, 510, 506, 511 and 505.

(All LSTs denoted thus * were crewed by the US Coast Guard)

LSTS-533 AND 27 UPLOADING FOR D-DAY. INTERESTINGLY LST-27 WAS CREWED BY THE US COAST GUARD, ONE OF ONLY FOUR SUCH VESSELS WITHIN TASK FORCE 126. (CRITICAL PAST)

A SERIES OF US HALF-TRACKS LOADING ONTO LST-28 AT POLGWYDDEN (TREBAH) HARD ON THE 1ST JUNE 1944. SOME 80 VEHICLES AND 471 PERSONNEL WERE LOADED PRIOR TO MOORING AT KING HARRY FERRY. LST-28 SAILED FOR NORMANDY WITH CONVOY B-3. (CRITICAL PAST)

The convoys for Force B sailed from a number of different ports and harbours once loaded. Their numbers were also increased with the addition of both LCTs, LCI(L)s and the tows out of Falmouth. With H-Hour being 06.30 on D-Day, the three Cornish convoys making up Force B sailed as follows:

Convoy B-1 – sailed from Plymouth and Fowey with a total of 14 x LSTs and 46 x LCTs from the former and 4 x LSTs from the latter.

Convoy B-2 – sailed from Plymouth with a total of 32 x LSTs, 46 x LCTs and 6 x LCI(L)s, the latter to sail at the head of the convoy as it was destined to land as quickly as possible on OMAHA Beach.

Convoy B-3 – sailed from Falmouth, Helford and Fowey, with a total of 34 x LSTs with the Falmouth vessels towing a total 42 x tows.

Each craft was ordered to carry sufficient fuel to ensure that on landing in Normandy, the LST had the correct trim.

The first attempt to launch the invasion was delayed by General Eisenhower for 24 hours due to stormy weather. Eisenhower's last minute and bold decision to go was always fraught with danger as the landings on OMAHA Beach demonstrated. Throughout the 6th June, he carried a small piece of paper in his jacket pocket.

TROOPS OF 30TH CHEMICAL DECONTAMINATION
COMPANY, 5TH SPECIAL ENGINEER BRIGADE
'LOCKED DOWN' ON BOARD LST-325. THE LARGE
BOARD WITH '474 O' IS AN ARMY LOADING SERIAL
NUMBER, WITH THE 'O' DENOTING OMAHA BEACH.
ST MAWES CASTLE CAN BE SEEN IN THE RIGHT-
BACKGROUND OF THE PHOTOGRAPH AND THE
FLY WHEEL AND CABLE ATTACHMENT AT THE
BOTTOM OF THE PICTURE ARE THE LST'S BALLOON
TETHERING MECHANISM. (US NAVAL HISTORY &
HERITAGE COMMAND)

On it he had written the following;

"Our landings in the Cherbourg-Havre area have failed to gain a satisfactory foothold and I
have withdrawn the troops. My decision to attack at this time and place was based upon the best
information available. The troops, the air and the Navy did all that Bravery and direction to duty
could do. If any blame is found attached to this attempt it is mine alone."

Eisenhower had been so nervous at the time that he dated it the 5th July.

As the Allies pushed on in France bases were established. At this point, SBS and
its Districts turned their hand to Plan RHUMBA, a reverse-BOLERO in which many
installations and personnel were released back to their previous owners and
employers

For Cornwall, the launch of the invasion really saw the end of the county's
involvement. By the 1st October, USNAAB Falmouth turned itself wholly
over to the repair of landing ships and other naval craft damaged in action or
by storm. The Base history also suggests that there was a decline in morale
following the invasion; the excitement had gone to be replaced by monotony.